THE WORLD is full of wonderful things. The sun shines, the wind blows, the rain falls. We see a great flash of lightning and we hear the loud thunder. We put a seed in the ground and soon a plant may grow. We are part of a great, exciting universe. It is fun to know as much as we can about it.

Do you know

Why we need the sun?

Why the moon seems bright?

How green plants grow?

What your shadow is?

Have you ever wondered

What makes rain and rainbows?

How fish breathe under water?

Why giraffes have long necks?

Whether ostriches can fly?

In this book, Jeanne Bendick answers these questions and many others. You will have fun reading here about the world we live in. And you will have fun finding out even more things about the world by yourself, for there are many, many interesting things to see if we keep our eyes open.

Glenn O. Blough
Specialist in Elementary Science

McGRAW-HILL BOOK COMPANY
NEW YORK   LONDON   TORONTO

ALL AROUND YOU

A first look at the world

written and illustrated by
JEANNE BENDICK
foreword by GLENN O. BLOUGH

1 10

To all the good friends and critics who helped with this book—to Glenn O. Blough, Herman Schneider, Marguerita Rudolph, and all the other scientists and teachers who lent a hand; to all the parents who suggested material, and most of all to the boys and girls who knew what they wanted, my thanks.

FOURTEENTH PRINTING

ALL AROUND YOU

The world we live on is a big, big, BIG round ball. It is turning all the time, but you cannot see or feel this turning. There are other worlds, too, but the one we live on is called the Earth. It is made of soil and rock, trees and grass, air and water, and all the other things around you.

The sun shines on the earth, the rain falls on it, the wind blows over it. The sun shines on you, the rain falls on you, and the wind blows your hat off. You live on the earth, and everything around you is part of it.

THE DAY

Have you ever seen the day begin?   The dark sky starts to look brighter.   Then suddenly the sky is all pink and red and gold and even a little green.

The earth has turned until the sun is shining on the place where you are.   This is what makes it day.

THE SUN

The sun looks like a shiny gold plate, but it is really a big ball. It is glowing fiercely all the time, and its flames are much, much hotter and bigger than any fire you have ever seen.

The sun gives more light than all the electric lights in the world and more heat than all the furnaces. It is like a gigantic heater that keeps the earth warm. Without the sun, nothing would grow in the world.

The sun is farther away than the farthest place you have ever been. It is so far away that no one can go there, not even in the fastest rocket ever made.

THE NIGHT AND THE STARS

The sun is always shining. But it can only shine on one side of the earth at a time. It cannot light the side that is turned away from it. When the sun is shining on the other side of the world, it is night where you are.

At night, you can see the stars.

All day the stars are in the sky, but the light from the sun is so bright you cannot see them. When the sun is gone, the stars are bright enough to see. Stars look as tiny as pinheads, but some are even bigger than the sun. Big things look little when they are far away. In the sky, airplanes look like toys, but on the ground you can see that they are big. Stars are millions of times bigger than airplanes. They look very small because they are so far away. The sun is closer than the other stars, so it looks bigger.

THE MOON

The moon is a ball, too, like the earth and the sun. Sometimes it looks round and flat, like a plate. Sometimes it looks like half a plate, or like a thin slice of yellow melon. But whether you can see it or not, the moon is always round. Part of it looks dark because it is turned away from the sun.

The moon is smaller than the stars, but it is much nearer, so it looks bigger. And it has no light of its own. This sounds funny, but moonlight is only sunlight shining on the moon. You see the moon all lit up by this sunlight, even though the sun itself is out of sight.

SHADOWS

Do you know what a shadow is? A shadow is a place where no light shines. Do you know why no light shines there? Because something is in the way. If you are standing between the sun and the sidewalk, there is a place just your shape where the sun cannot shine, and that is your shadow.

Every shadow, whether it is yours or a tree's or the shadow of a skyscraper, is made the same way.

CLOUDS AND THE BLUE SKY AND RAINBOWS

When clouds float in front of the sun, they make shadows, too, because they keep sunlight from shining on the ground beneath them. Sometimes clouds look like cotton and sometimes they look like gray smoke, but really they are made of billions of tiny raindrops or bits of ice, so small and light that they float in the air like little balloons. All these raindrops or icedrops floating in a bunch make a cloud. Even when the whole sky looks gray with these clouds, the sun is still there above the gray raindrops.

On fine days the sky looks very blue. Sunlight is made of many colors and some of these colors are scattered through the air better than others. On clear days you can see blue shining from all over the sky.

Sometimes when the sun shines through millions of raindrops hanging in the air, we see all the colors of the sun's light—red, orange, yellow, green, blue, indigo, and violet—in a beautiful arch across the sky. We call that a rainbow. Perhaps you have seen little rainbows when sunlight shines into your soap bubbles.

AIR, WIND, THUNDER, AND LIGHTNING

All around the earth there is air. We breathe air, and so do other animals and plants. The sun shines through it, the clouds float in it. Air holds up birds and raindrops and airplanes.

When the air moves slowly, it is a breeze. When it moves faster, it is a wind. That is what wind is—air moving.

Sometimes when the wind blows very hard there is a storm. And sometimes thunder and lightning come with a storm. Do you know what lightning is? It is electricity in the sky. But electricity in the sky hasn't any wires to go through, so it has to jump from one place to another. A flash of lightning is electricity jumping—from cloud to cloud, or from a cloud to the ground.

Lightning heats the air through which it goes, making that air swell up. This causes the big noise that is thunder.

FOG AND RAIN

Sometimes the clouds are very low, so low they touch the ground and wrap themselves around the trees and float above the water. We call that fog, or mist.

When the tiny drops of water that make clouds or fog get very close together they join and make bigger drops. These drops are too heavy to float in the air, so they fall down. And that is rain.

THE YEAR

A year is a long time—as long as it takes the earth to go around the sun, as long as from one birthday to another. Lots of things happen in a year—one Easter, one Thanksgiving, one Christmas, one spring, one summer, one autumn, and one winter.

Spring is the morning of the year, when everything wakes up. Leaves pop out of the trees, flower plants come out of the ground, and animals that have slept all winter pop out of their holes. Spring is the time for planting. Then the ground is soft and warm from the rain and the sun.

Summer is the daytime of the year. It is the time for growing. The sunshine is hot and bright and all the growing things stretch up to meet it. Plants cannot be strong and healthy without the sun. Flowers get bright and fruits get ripe. Birds sing, and all kinds of things grow and stretch.

Autumn is the evening of the year, the harvest time. The last fruits and grains ripen and are picked. Some animals grow thicker coats, and they will be warm when winter comes. . Some animals store food. They will not be hungry when there is no food to find. Plants finish making their seeds. Leaves fall to the ground. After a while they crumble and become part of the soil.

Winter is the night time of the year, the time for resting. In cold places, gardens and fields rest, and so do seeds, waiting for the warmth of spring. Many animals rest in their caves and holes and hardly do a thing but breathe. This is the time of year when the days are short and the nights are very long.

SNOW

In some parts of the world it always stays warm, but in other places winter is the time of cold and snow and frozen things.

There is always water in the air. When the air is very cold, snowflakes fall instead of rain. Millions and millions of snowflakes come down, and no two are ever exactly alike.

SLEET, HAIL, AND ICE

Sometimes the raindrops freeze after they have started to fall.   If they freeze just a little bit, they are sleet.   And if they freeze into hard little balls, we call that hail. Sometimes hailstones have snow in them too.

Hail and sleet are frozen, snow is frozen, ice cream is frozen, and so is just plain ice.

Have you ever touched a piece of ice?

It is cold and hard and slippery.

If it is very thin, you can see through it, just as you can see through glass.

If it is thick, it is very strong—strong enough to skate on or build a house on.   But do you know what ice is?

It is water.

If you put ice in a warm place it will melt and you can see that it was only frozen water.

WATER

There is more water on the earth than anything else, more water than soil or rocks, wood or grass.

Some water falls to the earth as rain.

Some water comes up from springs underneath the ground.

Some of the water is in little brooks, small enough to hop across.

Some of it is in rivers, big enough to fish in, big enough to sail a boat on.

Some of the water is in lakes. It does not move so fast as the water in brooks and rivers. And some is in the wide, deep oceans, and this water is salty.

Some of the water from rivers, lakes, and oceans is soaked up by the warm air. You can see this happen when puddles on the sidewalks go away. The water has gone back into the air.

WATER EVERYWHERE

But water is not just in rivers and oceans and lakes, or in puddles you can see and things that feel wet. Water is in all growing things, and nothing can live without water just as nothing can live without sunlight. Water is in trees and flowers, in air and soil, and there is a lot of water in you.

Even if you haven't had a drink for a long time, there is a lot of water in you, in all parts of your body.

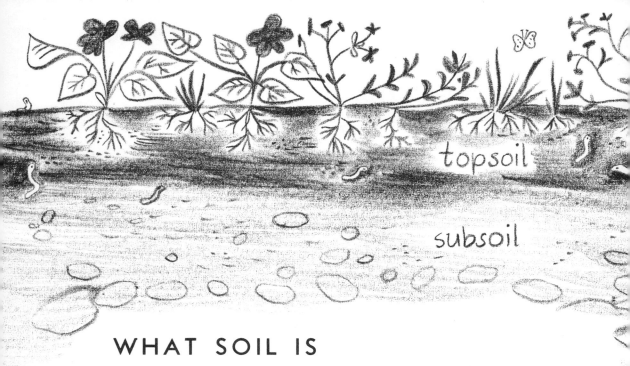

topsoil

subsoil

WHAT SOIL IS

Almost any place in the world, if you dig down deep enough, you will find rock. Over the top of most of this rock in the world there is spread a layer of soil, like icing on a cake. You may call it earth or dirt, but the real name is soil.

The top layer of this soil is not very deep—perhaps only several inches. But it is one of the most important things in the world. To grow well, plants need good topsoil.

Do you know what topsoil is made of?

First, it is made of rock—little pieces of rock. Wind and sun, ice and water, and plants have slowly broken big rocks up into little pieces. Then these little pieces of rock have become mixed with many other bits of things—crumbled pieces of dead plants and dried leaves, even dead insects and other dead animals.

In some places earthworms are helpful in making good soil. As they crawl through the earth getting their food, they make little tunnels that air and water come through. And they turn the soil over in such a way that rock pieces are slowly pushed to the top. Earthworms grind up the soil as they eat, and make it finer.

So the topsoil is bits of rock mixed with things that were once alive. These things in the topsoil that were once alive are called humus.

If you put some soil in a glass of water, you can separate these things. The rock, which is heavier, falls to the bottom of the glass.

The humus, which is made of lighter things, like crumpled leaves, floats on top.

UNDER THE GROUND

Above the ground you can see flowers and trees, animals running, bugs and birds flying, mountains sticking up through the clouds.

There are things under the ground, too.

Coal is under the ground in some places, and so is oil. Men bring the coal and oil up from underground. We can use coal and oil to heat houses, run trains and make the machinery in factories work.

In some places, beautiful stones called jewels are under the ground. In some places there is iron or gold, silver or tin.

Earthworms are under the ground nibbling the soil. And some animals have their homes underneath the ground. Gophers live in holes. Moles and woodchucks make themselves tunnels to run in.

Almost everything that grows out of the ground has roots underneath it. Roots reach out to get minerals and water from the earth for their plants. Trees have big roots. Other plants have smaller roots, but ones strong enough to hold them in place and get food from the soil.

Some roots do another job besides feeding their plants. They make a sort of net that helps hold the soil together. This keeps the soil from being washed away by heavy rains or blown away by strong winds.

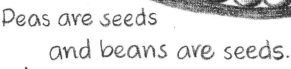
Nuts are seeds.

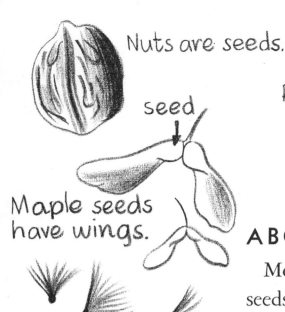

seed

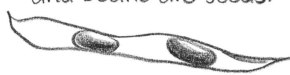
Peas are seeds
and beans are seeds.

Maple seeds
have wings.

Milkweed seeds sail
on parachutes.

ABOUT SEEDS

Most growing things come from seeds.

Plants have seeds, and new plants grow from these.

Trees drop seeds, and that is how new trees start.

Nuts are the seeds of some trees. They drop to the ground, and if the dirt covers them, or a squirrel buries them, new trees may grow from them.

The seeds of some trees have tiny wings, and they fly on the wind to far places before they fall to the ground and start to grow. Maple trees spread their seeds in this way. Some seeds, such as nuts, bounce to new places. Some, like milkweed seeds, sail on parachutes.

Every seed has a tiny plant in it and food for that plant.

Some, like pansy seeds, are shot out when their pods burst open. Some seeds from plants that grow near streams float away in the water. Animals carry seeds that stick to their fur, birds carry some, people even carry some.

Every seed has a little plant inside it, and food for that plant to grow on.

Every green plant in the world starts from a kind of seed. The tallest tree grows from a kind of seed. A blade of grass no bigger than a pin does, too.

Farmers plant radish seeds to get radish plants and corn seeds to get corn plants. Each kind of seed makes its own kind of plant.

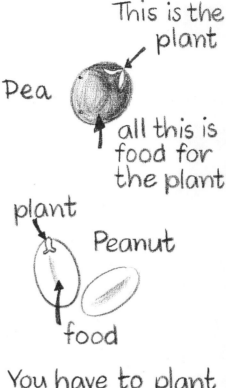

This is the plant

Pea

all this is food for the plant

plant

Peanut

food

You have to plant a corn seed to get corn

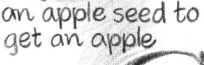

an apple seed to get an apple

a radish seed to get a radish

a cherry seed to get a cherry

PLANT FACTORIES

A blade of grass looks very small.   Most green leaves
look small, too.   But grass and leaves are really factories,
the smallest factories in the world.

They make their own food, inside themselves, and people or animals cannot do that.

Grass and leaves use the light from the sun

and something from the air

and the water and minerals their roots get from the earth

and they work with a special green material inside themselves, which is called chlorophyll. From these things green plants make all the food they need for living and growing. It's a very wonderful thing, and nobody knows exactly how they do it.

If the sun did not shine, plants could not make food.

If there were no water, plants could not make food.

If they did not have green chlorophyll, plants could not make food. There would be no cereal or fruit or vegetables. There would not be any meat, either. Do you know why? Because meat comes from animals that eat plants.

chlorophyll (clo-ro-fil)

WHERE PLANTS GROW

In all kinds of places plants are growing.

In hot, damp places where the sun shines most of the time and the soil is good, they grow very fast.

In cold, cold places, almost nothing grows but a little moss.

In very dry places nothing grows but some rough grass and maybe a little cactus.

So most plants need certain things to grow well—
warm sunshine and air
warm, fertile earth
and water.

Some plants grow wild wherever their seeds happen to fall. Where lots of trees grow, we have forests. Buttercups and berries grow in fields. Ferns and moss grow in shady places.

Some plants do not grow wild. We have to plant their seeds where we want them to grow.

Farmers plant their vegetables together in gardens, so they can take care of a lot of them at the same time. Farmers loosen the soil, so the plants can drink in plenty of water, and they pull out the weeds.

Farmers plant cherry trees together, or peach trees or pear trees. In a hot place, they may plant bananas. In a cool place, they may plant apples. Plants grow best in the kind of temperature they like.

Plants even grow in houses if you give them good soil and water and sun.

HOW PLANTS TAKE CARE OF THEMSELVES

All green plants store food for themselves and their seeds. Different plants store food in different places.

Potatoes are the underground stems of potato plants.

Some plants store food in their roots. Beets are the roots of beet plants.

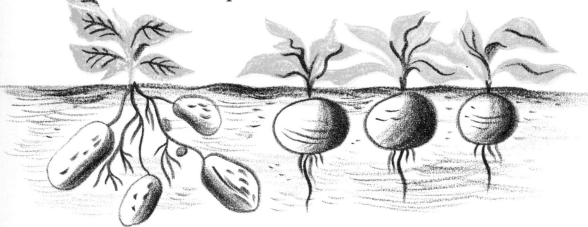

Some plants store food in bulbs before they stop growing. Then the leaves and the flowers of the plant die, but the bulb is ready to start growing again, to make a new plant. Tulips and daffodils make new plants this way. Onions are the bulbs of onion plants.

Many green plants die in the autumn when the ground gets cold and hard. Some just rest until spring comes again.

Some trees lose their leaves in the autumn. One reason is to save water. When the ground gets cold, the roots of the tree have a hard time getting water from the earth. Green leaves would give off a lot of this water to the air. If the leaves are gone, the tree can keep its water for itself.

When the leaves stop making food for their trees, the green color goes out. Then some leaves look yellow. The yellow was there all the time, but you could not see it until the green faded. The leaves of other trees look red. Those leaves started making the red when they stopped making food. Leaf stems get dry at the place where they join the branch, and the wind blows the leaves off.

Some trees, the kind we call evergreens, have long, thin, needlelike leaves that come off only a few at a time. So evergreens look green all winter.

In the winter, some trees look cold and dead, but all the time a special juice called sap is in the trunk of the tree. When spring comes, the sap starts moving up through the tree and into the branches. It feeds every twig and bud.

First the buds look like little brown bumps.

Then they look like pink and green bumps.

Finally each bump unfolds and becomes a leaf or a flower.

THE ANIMALS CALLED MAMMALS

The world is full of animals,
big ones like elephants,
little ones like mice,
and smart ones like people.
Animals that swim, like whales,
animals that fly, like bats,
and animals that dance, like people.

Many of the animals we know are called mammals. Most mammals are born alive. Very few pop out of eggs, the way birds or fish do. All mammals have either hair or fur. And mammal mothers have milk to give their babies.

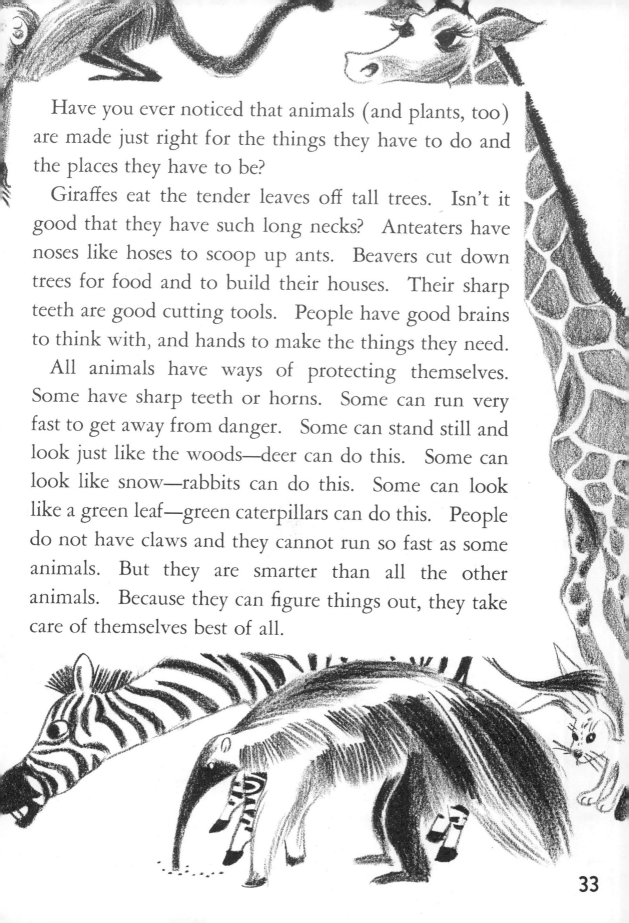

Have you ever noticed that animals (and plants, too) are made just right for the things they have to do and the places they have to be?

Giraffes eat the tender leaves off tall trees. Isn't it good that they have such long necks? Anteaters have noses like hoses to scoop up ants. Beavers cut down trees for food and to build their houses. Their sharp teeth are good cutting tools. People have good brains to think with, and hands to make the things they need.

All animals have ways of protecting themselves. Some have sharp teeth or horns. Some can run very fast to get away from danger. Some can stand still and look just like the woods—deer can do this. Some can look like snow—rabbits can do this. Some can look like a green leaf—green caterpillars can do this. People do not have claws and they cannot run so fast as some animals. But they are smarter than all the other animals. Because they can figure things out, they take care of themselves best of all.

ANIMALS THAT LIVE IN WATER

Many kinds of animals live in water. Some swimming mammals live there, coasting along near the top, so they can stick their heads up and breathe the air.

Fish live in water, and they can breathe without coming to the top because they have a special way of breathing through gills. Fish are animals, too.

Some sea animals are no bigger than your littlest fingernail and some, like sharks, may be as big as a boat.

Some sea animals live so deep in the ocean that people almost never see them. Some swim along almost on top.

Some live in hard shells, growing onto rocks or on the bottom, and never move.

Some, like lobsters and crabs, live in shells with their feet sticking out so they can walk along the bottom.

Some fish eat the plants that grow in water. Some fish eat other fish. Some fish jump out of the water to catch the little insects flying just above it.

Starfish look like stars, sea horses look like tiny horses, coral looks like great trees, butterfly fish look like butterflies, and some fish look like little lights. And there are some sea animals that look like beautiful flowers and some that look like bubbles.

AMPHIBIANS AND REPTILES

Long ago, there were only tiny animals in the world. They all lived and breathed in the water, and nothing at all lived on land. As millions of years went by, some of these animals slowly changed so they could breathe air. Then they could move out of the water onto the land.

First they have tails—

then they grow legs.

The tails disappear

And here's a grown-up amphibian!
(am·fib′·i·an)

There are animals nowadays that change from breathing under water to breathing air on land. When they are young they have tails instead of legs, and they swim under water like fish. When these animals grow bigger, their tails disappear and they grow legs instead. Their gills, which are the things that let them breathe under water, disappear and lungs grow instead. With lungs they can breathe on land.

These animals have a long name—amphibians. Frogs are amphibians. Amphibians never get far away from water, because they need things very damp.

snakes

Some animals of the reptile family live partly in the water and partly on land, but they always breathe air. Reptiles have short little legs or no legs at all. They are cold-blooded like fish, but they always have lungs like mammals. And even if they live in the water, they lay their eggs on land.

Turtles are reptiles, and so are alligators and crocodiles and lizards and snakes. While most reptiles like to be near the water, others can live on dry, dry land.

All these animals are REPTILES.

turtles

crocodiles

gila monsters

chameleons and lizards

alligators

BIRDS

Birds live almost everywhere in the world. The hot, damp jungles are full of brightly colored birds—parrots and parakeets, cockatoos and macaws. The cold, snowy places near the South Pole have birds, too—black and white penguins.

All birds have feathers, and no other animals do.

All birds hatch out of eggs.

All birds have wings, but some can't fly. The wings on penguins and ostriches are too small to hold them up.

Many birds live in trees. They build their nests there and lay their eggs in the nests. When baby birds hatch, the tree is their safe home until their wings are strong enough for them to fly away.

Some birds make their nests in the fields, deep in the tall grass.

Some like to be around houses. They build their nests where the roof hangs over, or even in the chimney.

Chickens are birds, and they usually live in chicken houses. Ducks and turkeys are birds, too. Some ducks and turkeys live in farmyards, and others are wild birds that live in the woods and fields.

crickets

ladybugs

flies

INSECTS

You probably call the little flying, creeping, crawling things you see just bugs. But their right name is insects.

Insects live in bushes and grass and trees, in fields and houses and in the ground. Some even live on other animals.

Did you know that there are more insects in the world than any other kind of animal? They fly and hop and crawl and dig. Some insects, the ants, build hills and cities of their own. Insects called silkworms spin silk. Bees make honey. And crickets make music with their feet.

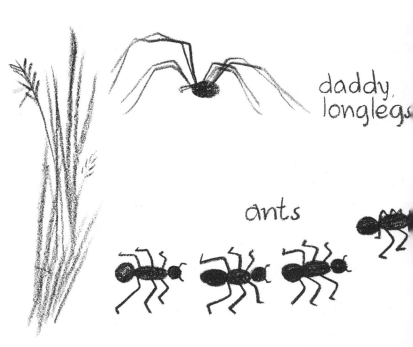

daddy longlegs

ants

All these (and many more) are insects.

Lots of insects grow up in a curious way. When they are little, they look like tiny worms, and most of their lives are spent in just growing. Mosquitoes start this way, and so do beetles and flies, ants and bees. Some caterpillars grow into butterflies. Other wormlike wriggling things become moths. So all insects do not look the same. Worms in fruit are insects. So are caterpillars and potato beetles, flies and moths.

The things that some insects do are helpful to people. They spin silk and make honey and help the flowers to make seeds. Some insects are pests. They bite and sting and eat our plants and clothes, food and even furniture. Insects are everywhere.

bees

and moths

mosquitoes

and caterpillars

41

ALL LIVING THINGS GROW

You may not look like a bug or a plant or a bird, but in a lot of ways you are just like them. You and all other living things need air and water, food and rest. You are growing all the time. All living things grow.

Plants and birds, fish, insects, and mammals all start out little and they all grow. They grow during the day and they grow all night.

Insects grow. They grow new skins, and some even grow wings.

Plants grow bigger. They grow new leaves and flowers, fruit and nuts.

Sea creatures grow bigger. Some grow new shells and some even grow new claws after one has been lost.

Birds grow bigger. Their wings grow big and strong enough to carry them through the air.

Mammals grow bigger. They grow new hair or fur. Some grow new teeth and some grow new horns.

You are growing all the time, too. You are born no bigger than a doll, and you grow until you are a man or woman. You grow during the day and when you are asleep—when the sun is shining or when it is snowing. Even when you are grown up, parts of you keep growing. Your hair and your nails grow. Your skin grows as it wears out, or to fix a place where it has been hurt. Growing never stops.

You need things to help you grow, just as everything around you does.

You need good clean air to breathe, and sunshine and food to eat. If you live in a cool place, you must have clothes and a house to keep you warm.

You need water to drink. We get our drinking water from rain that has fallen into lakes and rivers, or has soaked down into springs under the earth.

The world around you is full of the things you need.

You eat food that plants have made. They make fruit and nuts, melons and berries, sugar from beets and sugar cane and maple trees. You eat the roots and stems of some plants, the leaves and seeds of others. These things that plants have made become part of you.

Animals give you food, too—fish and meat, milk and eggs.

Your woolen coat and leather shoes also came from animals. Your house and furniture may be made of wood from trees.

The cotton for your shirt grew around the seeds of a cotton plant. The linen for your handkerchief was once the stem of a flax plant. If you have a silk scarf, a silkworm made the silk thread.

People weave these things into cloth, but plants and animals made them.

And if there is a feather in your hat, it came from a bird.

The world is all around you. All day long you feel things—warm sunshine, or snow on your cheeks, wind blowing in your hair, damp earth.

You smell the sweet air after a spring rain, flowers in the summer sun, and leaves burning in the fall. And in the winter there is the wet smell of your woolen coat, the good smell of Thanksgiving dinner, and the nice, sharp smell of Christmas trees.

You taste cool water and sweet honey, sour pickles and salty peanuts.

You hear the birds singing and dogs barking, the wind sighing, and your friends calling.

You see the blue sky and the gray rain, the black night and the shiny stars, spider webs and snowflakes, bees and trees, rainbows and mountains, and sea and sunshine.

These things are the world, and they are all around you.